PROPHECIES & TRANSFORMATIONS
by Kosrof Chantikian

KOSMOS
SAN FRANCISCO
1978

Some of these poems first appeared or will appear in: *Blue Unicorn*, *Green House*, *Kosmos* and *Literary Tabloid*.

Library of Congress Catalog Card Number: 75-35012

ISBN: 0-916426-01-7

Cover design by Christin Couture.
Typesetting by Katie O. Flynn & Steve Oglethorpe
    (Pacific Sun Typography)

Modern Poets Series
First Printing – January of the Full Moon 1978.

for Atamant & Marna
again

CONTENTS

TRANSFORMATIONS – PROPHECIES

CONTENTS

PROPHECIES - TRANSFORMATIONS

TRANSFORMATIONS – PROPHECIES

transformation lays the ground for prophecy

& prophecy is the Poet's transmuting invention

to transform is to be transformed

for example, the Poet as Seer prophecies

Love will always refuse to die!

BEGINNINGS OF KNOWLEDGE

if you take Wisdom from Laughter
        or the Sun from Moon
        or the Eyes & Face from a Child
        or the Horn from a Unicorn
        or the Umbilical Cord of the Unborn

        or Egypt from Kleopatra
        or the Evening from Morning Star
        or Love from Love Making
        or Red from the Sundown

if you separate Gertrude from Stein
        or Whitman from America
        or Dreams from Night
        or Light from Shadow
        or Man from Woman

        or Woman from Man
        or Children from Trees
        or Laughter from the Body
        or Body from the Mind

if you abolish Iris from her Rainbow
        or Air from Breathing
        or to Be from Is
        or Knowing from Doing
        or Desire from Thighs

        or Sokrates from Philosophy
        or Diana from the Moon
        or Blake from Prophecy
        or Intuition from Eyes

if you do this
if you cut up & mutilate
if you destroy
if you take

>   the World from itself
>   or Perception from the Senses
>   or Memory from its future
>   or Dance from Poetry
>   or Poetry from Language
>   or Language from Thought
>   or Song from Existence

>   or Kissing from your Lips
>   or Breast from your Body
>   or the Erotic from yourself
>   or my Tongue from all of you
>   or your Eyes from mine

then listen

>   the Imagination rising
>   from the ashes of itself
>   will make all the World
>   whole again & again

"these are the beginnings of knowledge"
>   the Poet said

TO THE RAIN

the way you fly to sounds of her mouth
from your red cloud home
bursting upon her
electric belly thighs

your night fingers of song
feeling her black pulse
roll over this cracked skin
oiling it smooth into dreams of orange clay

& yearning for every piece of dust
& every worm
she bends a blue light

as it passes by
swallowing every movement
every touch of the color of sky

NIGHT

Time summons Night
after paying Day
a day's wages

Day goes home
to rest
it is Night's turn now

to cover the Sky
to lay down with the
Moon

yet when Night comes
only the Morning Star
will not yawn

for the Morning Star
it makes no difference at all
how it is perceived

it is enough to know
that the Evening Star
is the only member of heaven

over which Time
has merely
a semantic influence

MOMENTS IN THE LIFE OF A SPIDER

I watch Spring in my garden
conspire with the wind & rain
to catch a spider by surprise

her legs
now grasping for the air
know better than to resist

& beginning her descent
falling down
across a window pane

she does not pretend to understand
curvature of space is the cause
of gravity pulling her to the ground

having found a dead large ant
shriveled & rotting against a glass pane
she has already become aware of her fate

LOVING WITH YOU

in bed
my hip touches
your body sleeping warm

through an open window
I see a yellow jack
circle over a patch of wild flowers

a green bird flies by
its wings out wide as if it held
the whole sky & the leaves of this tree

I watch how they move
at the wind's invitation to dance
its fingers singing

my desire is gone now
I see only your winter eyes
& the thin charm of your throat

I imagine how it would be
if we should some day find in a floating dream
exploding in our brain

a hunger for thighs
inviting colors of purple sounds
to touch all of ourselves

TO WALT WHITMAN

Celebrating the sky
I hear a chorus of birds
I see a dance of trees of grass
everything living growing
in wild expectation of itself

I see a butterfly
who brushes past me
in search of a flower

I hear clouds moving endlessly in the sky
whose perpetual motion
endures even greater than the
second law of thermodynamics

I taste the sun
whose light energy feeds our body
I eat the moon
night flower of my Imagination

I hear a poplar
who dances to me her desire
in the afternoon shade

& I see a red bird
flying freely through the breeze
wondering when she will free all caged prisoners
& destroy the zoos of captivity

Celebrating the sky
I hear a chorus of birds
I see a dance of trees of grass
everything living growing
in wild expectation of itself

MORNING REVERIE

Celebration will never end
as long as the Will
wills to love
(except if birds refuse to fly)

Love can never die
or be forgotten
(unless change remains the same)

Celebration will never end
& dreams one day
(will not always stay so)

PERCEPTION OF MY BEING

I am the Wind Rain
& Sea

I am the Sun
& Moon

I am the leaves silently
whispering into the Poet's Eye

I am the Bird of Life
Death is seeking

I am Fire
whose Energy serenades your Naked Body

I am Night
transforming myself to Day

I am a Heart & Thought
no power can ever unbind

I am a Rose Blue
Imagine who I am

do not presume about my life
without looking & touching me

I am Energy
equivalent to the mass of the Imagination alone

look at me
my Eyes

taste me   feel me
come to know who I am

above all
listen to me   my Eyes

I am the Wind Rain
& Sea

SECOND CONVERSATION WITH RAIN

tell me
do you dance intentionally
or is that choice
no longer yours

was it ever
was it ever possible
for you to refuse

to curse gravity
to say no
to think of yourself
to save yourself
        for yourself

or do you
exist merely for pleasure

dance then
dance with my face
& I will touch the whole of your
        s k y

TRANSFORMATIONS

in the meadow a tree grows
a bird flies past me
rain falls on my fingers

the lonely wail
the old die like left over
thanksgiving dinner

babes are born
snow forms on my lips
lovers meet anywhere

present moments now
overwhelm the weak
failures of the past

at last
the new moon
fills the sky so amazingly

THE MOON FLOWER DEAD

> "I say Live, Live because of the Sun"
>   – Anne Sexton   *Live or Die*

they say you killed yourself Anne
the new york times gang says so
even some of your friends

Anne
you with eyes pulsating energy
slicing through a moderator's stale questions
about why & why
do you write poetry

you Poet Anne
dead
as critics pay you tributes now
like amazon leeches sucking
a poem's left over blood

all these obituaries laughing in your face
& you Sister Anne you knew so well

'Live' you had once told us
'Live because of the Sun'

Anne Poet Anne
you knew so much more
than the rest of us
& yet you once told us
you wished you had had an education

Anne Anne
be serious
you knew so much more
than the rest of us

you with your fingers dancing in the air
holding the nicotine poison
between your lips
puffing out poems
of how lonely it's possible to be
like a spider despised by its own web

what is death like Poet Anne
are things more quiet now
has death released your dreams
does memory explode
does it disappear
is this why death is so wonderful
does it erase the chalk nerve endings in the brain
does it make the heart numb

'Live' you had once told us
'Live because of the Sun'

Anne Sister Anne
we live
we live because of the Sun
          & Moon & Wind

Poet Anne
we live because of you Anne
we live because of ourselves

'Live' you had once told us
'Live because of the Sun'

Anne Poet Anne
tell me
who murdered you

IN BED WITH THE FULL MOON

wind trembling
trees quaking
ground howling
ghosts of my memory in an autumn sky

outside my window
the Moon
falling down upon me

Diana
constant gazer of Earth & I
protect these cold bones of mine

I who no longer fear the loneliness of sky
I who have lost lovers in my dreams
I whom time has abandoned

I who laugh at nightmares
of stomachs exploding
& touch my wet dreams inventing words

'these are not laughing matters'
        you say undressing me

Moon Diana
I know

who is fool enough to live
not able to laugh

at what has been
at the past
what was

APHRODITE'S REBIRTH

after a painting by
Sandro Botticelli

from a kosmic shell
bursting from
time's womb
you emerge

you
giver of love
appear in a lake of green song
at the edge of a forest

there waiting impatiently
the wind
impersonating an angel
blows for you

wild roses the color of morning
celebrating your birth
your reappearance
in the world

LETTER TO EMILY DICKINSON

Emily Dickinson
do you know Emily
        about yourself
the way I do
the way I do this moment

your hair split in two
& eyes that smile
lips that say
here   now   this instant

I see you
were you really so shy Emily
as shy as they say you were

you smile at me
as though you knew I were the black wind
about to enter your face

I know you Emily
        you rolled up hills
& touched atoms of my breath
        with winks & turns of your mouth

Emily
        you were so alone
that you asked a stranger
        if your verse is 'alive'

at 32 you were unsure of yourself
        your poetry
& thinking that 'the mind is so near
        itself it cannot see distinctly'

you wondered whether your poems
        had a pulse & breathed life
into a world that could not
        imagine your existence

& what did he write
        you Emily

you wanted to know
if your poetry was alive

instead he asked your age
        & what books you read
                & who your companions were

Emily
as always
revealing yourself
brought a fool's reply

how could he understand
        you Emily
when you said
        that your companions were hills
                & the sundown
                        and a dog as large as yourself

NEFERTITI

there is a picture
of a woman on my desk
whose Eyes are older
than the earth's crust
whose Ears hear
the roar of futile tongues
& whose Lips say to me

You Poets - what do you do each day

Be aware of your power

develop patience

nourish Intuition

Sing more often

touch your Eyes

step outside your mortal Body

Kiss your Lips

put your Tongue deliciously inside yourself

You who Are & who Sing

You who Sing & who Are

APRIL DREAM

standing on one leg
with no clothes on
my hands flying toward the sky

my face melting
stones running toward me
I heard a red swan sing

> better to die laughing in the accuser's face
> throwing poems in their lead eyes
> better to spit in fate's mouth
> better to sing love will never die
> than confess the Sun is a traitor

the red swan looked at me
her eyes streaking space
with the color of afternoon laughter

a moment later she flew away
I could see those red wings
flapping toward the Sun

she disappeared
suddenly I realized
the red swan was the Sun

MOTHER

my Mother
in her garden
pulling out
the weeds
          the perpetual crab grass

kneeling down over her flowers
gently touching
this leaf
a bush of red sky azaleas

my Mother
seventy-one   her hair
the color of the
Arctic Wind

she calls to me
with her hands
&
eyes now

I walk
over to her
touching my hand
to her shoulder

she points to a new born flower
with the spade
in her hand
fire flies begin to light the coming night

she speaks in Armenian
I watch the movement of her mouth
as her lips
transform the air into colors of ancient vowels

I touch my face to this flower
forcing time to recede
compelling it to carry me my dreams
to this moment I was born

in my Mother's bed
watching her eyes
smelling the color of her ochre hair
it wasn't the ancient landscape of the
            Arctic Wind then

TO MICHELANGELO
1475–1975

archangel they called you
    do you remember your birth

sent away to suck
    the blue milk of a stone cutter

you became you were always becoming
    Michelangelo Sculptor in Florence & Rome

each time you touched stone
    your fingers invented poems

at will your hands kissed
    transforming marble to form

but you died losing to time
    leaving centuries of rock

to dream
    of your hands

CONVERSATION WITH YOU

we spoke tonight
about death

you asked if I had sometime thought
of dying

& yes – I recalled
looking at a pale

reflection of myself in a bathroom mirror
this morning when I awoke

the skin under my eyes
how heavier had it grown

but then laughing
wild with the black moon

as she undressed herself
& took me to where the sky

already naked
whispered I needn't be afraid

MY EYES

it is not until I have gotten off
that I see this is the wrong stop
I look around quickly

dazed   the bars howl
trying to intoxicate
the night with brutal sound

in the ghetto I see
small red mouths call out
"white man   there's a white man"

here even the air is against me
the black fog
with its devouring mask

with its knuckles & fists
soon it will be my turn
to be eaten

my Intuition
has already prophesied
this evening's main event

I am carrying poetry books
but instead of song
they are filled with lead

my feet stick to the ground's laughing sweat
I am drowning in cement
"a white man   a white man"

how can I scream back
how shall I yell concerning
the origins of my blood

Armenia   Asia Minor
link between two continents
caught squeezed

into submission
between Europe & Asia
my being my blood

a memory of Mark Antony
Armenian army deserts him
Octavian wins

& Kleopatra a Greek
Queen of the Nile
how do I scream about this my blood

to these two ghetto pimps
who assume they know me
the color of my blood

my heart begins to fly faster than morning light
invading absolute space
the ground dissolves into my knees

it is here in the caves of night
where even time shrinks in fear
that we touch & taste the limits of ourselves

it is here where even
the wind dare not move
too visibly

that I discover
what I will allow
& what I will refuse

my money taken
& the poetry books smashed
against a laughing wall

it is my body
now they demand
I have a choice

these pimps say
either my sex
or a bullet in my face

I have always loved two things
Love
& the clinging Night

but now
even the Moon
has abandoned me

in the end
it is my Eyes that save
my Poet's Eyes

for they have never seen
Eyes like mine
Eyes of Europe & Asia combined

they leave me running
down & down into their tombs
back to their future their catacombs

my clothes scattered
my poetry silent on the ground
the *I Ching* I carried

in my hands all the way to Teotihuacán
& Mayan Tikal
looks at me perseveringly   saying

"the superior person
takes thought of misfortune
& arms against it in advance"

at home
it does no good
to look at my Eyes in a glass

I touch them very slowly
like dawn walking among the trees

my Eyes   my Eyes
Song the Night
forever my Eyes

VISION OF MY BODY

my body
      which I dreamed of before birth

which knows the wind's embrace
      & is inseparable

from my mind the moon
      & wonders what goes on in heaven

loves above all you
      & the night

my body
      which dreams of your orange breasts

eating the sun
      & which is no different from my soul

searches for your kisses
      like rain hunting the earth   &

my body
      which invents red stars

in the morning breeze
      for you

SEXUALITY

an azure sky of lust
in my body
that I feel

I hold myself
warmly under a quilt
hand made

it is morning
the wind is up
but I remain in bed

lust makes me stay
my dreams remind me of white nights
colors that would devour any heaven or hell

what is a sexual meal
what poets most crave
flesh or is it words

or words sunk so deeply into flesh
that to eat one
would be like biting the other

TO A WOMAN

your breast is
the Imagination
laughing in purple autumns

your breast is
the torrid antarctic eating
black poems upon moonrays

TO A FRIEND

it is not merely
that red harps you touch
burn the air

but your Eyes
that are

sensations in my finger bones
dissolving loneliness
into its grave

BODY & SOUL

                    a love song

I will tell you with only words
          a language an invention of myself
about you

poems that run down time
          but each time elude me
like the fingers of a bird slicing morning air

syllables that touch our bodies
          like electrified dreams of red nights
phrases that leap out of black stars

that dance kissing us
          while our voices sing
to the earth's laughter urging us on & on

delight of your
          blue eyebrows
& your autumn face

I feed you rubies of nectar
          & eat them with you   each one slowly
I dream of green roses undressing the sun

. . . .

galaxies were born & died
          before body touched its soul
& soul began to sing to its body

now we have the wind's knowledge –
          become song

. . . .

when you kiss my body
time must pause to reinvent itself

when you collide against my skin
the moon's dreams burst open orange nights

when your hands hold me everywhere
the last fossil remains

of my nightmares
crumble beneath your fire skin

you are the Night of Asia
& I am the moon dancing in your mouth

you are fire singing
in the core of stars

I feed you rubies of nectar
& eat them with you   each one slowly

WOMAN WITH MANGO

after a painting by
Gauguin

Vahine of the South Seas
black woman with red eyes
floating through islands of purple midnights

I can feel your whole April face thinking
when shall we eat this blood ripe mango
you are holding in your hand

you are standing on your dreams
in his studio
while he paints you

because you wish you were floating
on waves
instead of having to pose

for so long
while the morning sun
waits for you to come onto the beach

& the sand wonders
how your red eyes & evening lips
can be trained to be so still

I touch your earth face
your black moon hair
your belly overflowing

& now I am certain you know
how better it would be to stop
leave that studio

& run undressing
into the morning surf
where palm tree waters

of the sea
await your body's
beginning touch

SONG TO MYSELF & TO YOU

I am nothing
I am everything
I am an instant
I am forever
I am death
I contain myself in myself
I am life

. . . .

I am winter laughter
& a taste of morning waves in spring
I am movement of black sound into orange nights
I am the Full Moon at the end of January

. . . .

I invent children
who stop the sky's bleeding

I invent your body
from dreams of green stars

& the end of all tomorrows
with touches of your evening breasts

I invent you & the word
longing for nights to burn

I invent tongues dreaming
of sea winds in hollow caves

I invent you – the Dance – with sapphire hair
I invent Song which invents the world

I tie boredom & lies
round each other with barbed wire

where they corrode in hissing slime
to the morning chants of red birds

I invent Eyes
which invent me each day

I invent silence & the sky asleep
& laughter where our thighs will meet

I invent signs which decimate pity
& hope which laughs down despair

I invent bodies which embrace words
no less than love

& I invent words colors smells music of silence
red mornings odors of your sex

flowers which bloom
only in the night

I invent the Kiss
which flies searching for you everywhere

in jugular oceans in frozen jungles
in drowning deserts of solitude

I invent Memory
which knows where you hide

I invent your Face & mine
which meet graze & become magnetized

I invent Desire
which invents itself

I invent a new History
where all is Poem

      where future ends

          where time exists only now

             in your Eyes

& each time I touch your body
I invent myself

      the sky   an autumn dawn   a new time

I invent Love
which invents everything

& I invent you & the Night
& myself every day

PROPHECIES – TRANSFORMATIONS

La première étude de l'homme qui veut être
poëte est sa propre connaissance, entière;
il cherche son âme, il l'inspecte, il la tente,
l'apprend. Dès qu'il la sait, il doit la
cultiver!

. . . .

Je dis qu'il faut être *voyant*, se faire *voyant*.

– Rimbaud

The first study of the person who wants to be
a poet is the knowledge of themself, complete.
One looks for one's soul, inspects it, tests it,
learns it. As soon as one knows it, one must
cultivate it!

. . . .

I say one must be a *seer*, make oneself a *seer*.

BEGINNING LOVE SONG

when I begin to Sing
you will leave your bare
tin typewriters

throw those files away
& burn the morning
carbon copies of nothing

& when I touch my fingers
to your lips
you will remember about yourself

the wind
waves & leaves
flying in the spring

when I kiss you
& you me

when our thighs unclothe themselves
making offices begin to melt

you will touch
your eye to all of myself
& the World will begin

POET'S PROPHECY

if dogs bark
as frequently as people
say nothing when they speak

& the Morning Star
accuses the Evening
of conspiracy with the Sky

if a Raindrop
sues its wetness
in the hope of advancement

& the Sun becomes
jealous of the Moon's
presence in the Night

if the Wind
decides to have no further
dealings with the Atmosphere

& Songs indict Sound
on grounds of infidelity

if violins can no longer
live with their bows

& Waves regard
the Ocean with contempt

if the egg vomits
at the sight of sperm

& fetus declines to be Born
having become too attached
to its Umbilical Cord

if Mouth condemns
Tongue for dreaming unheard
of wet Dreams

& Love sleeps
serenely with untruth in bed

then we'll consider
signing petitions

to commit Beauty
& tear Revolution to shreds

but not
until then

THE POET & THE CROW

seasons change
leaves fall from
their mother trees

big black crows chant
melodies of irritation
at poets singing poems under trees

this crow having
wrongly concluded I'm hamming in
lifts its wings from a tall oak

& flies toward that evergreen
for a better look at me

the poet & the crow
one desiring to fly
the other to sing

meet become acquainted
listen
& decide to help one another do both

the poet & the crow
lovers in another time
where Asia & Europe always meet

aware of each other's
hungry gaze
rip off their clothes

who will fly
& who will sing
will exist loving fall & spring

SONG IS EXISTENCE

> "Gesang ist Dasein"
> – Rilke   *Sonnets to Orpheus*

the hated past will crumble soon
to morning reveries of sky
of poplars wishing for night's embrace

of future kisses
searching lips'
grounding touch

the hated past will crumble soon
to the World's
recollection of its Body

which is Song
& Song
is to Be

ON THE WAY TO SAN FRANCISCO

39000 feet surrounded
by a planet sky

carved parceled fenced in
a nation enveloped by tv anthills
      & spray can history

to the right a horizon of sound
a residue of the Poet's Imagination
to leap into this marsh of cloud

to saw off this wing of black ice
to see how deeply the tongues
of this mass of people in a moment

dissolve like volcanic snow
into a panic of naked dreams
dancing with autumn's orange laughter

JOURNEY TO TEOTIHUACÁN

I

55

I stand in the courtyard of a cloister
birds sing
the sun whispers to unknown plants

a retreat from the world of machines
hairdryers & electric ass wipers

built in the seventeenth century
deserted now
except for the sun plants & birds

I linger for a moment
for renewal
to remember   to relearn

the meaning of silence
the origin of sound
produced by the wind

the language of sky
before the world's inauguration
before the birth

walking inside the cloister I hear
a room of rocks   lips   faces
monks turned to stone

from their continual negation of song
I do not attempt to speak here

II

outside again I am beside what used to be
a nun   una monja
now a sunflower

I watch now as a bee sucks this sunflower
sucking the nun

after a thousand years
of withdrawing from the Wind

now at last a flower of the Sun
she sucks her lips
on the body of a yellow-striped bee

III

Moon Pyramid
lying here with you
in each other

with memories of Poetry
& wretched priests who cast me out
now I return

armed with phrases
words
syllables of red nights

I give you my love
feed me in return

a Poet hungry for your raw words

IV

standing on top of the sun Pyramid
alone except for the clouds
the lost Toltec dreams

alone where the earth returns to Song
where the Poet licks the color of the Wind

visible for the first time I see it & touch it
my body disappears into its mist
            the odor of its sex

I am no longer flesh
nor bones nor nightmares of solitude
only the sound of my Eye moving

V

Sun Moon & Wind
we are all one
moving toward each other

moving toward what we might become
by dancing & eating a past that has
brought us to this primordial part of ourselves

we are moving toward a time
when the Imagination & the Body
will be recognized
as (whole embodiments of) one

INNOCENCE

when you kiss my lips
the sky is red

when you dance upon the earth
the moon is born again

when your fingers of light
close my eyes
I still see you

& when you take my body
to yours
the world is a song of delight

EXPERIENCE

the past will be respected if we can
taste
what it has been

a past which barricades
laughter
will never endure

REALITY BEGINNING WITH A FANTASY

dreams of you floating
in azure skies

your green hair flies from
the earth

but it is the thinness of your thighs
I will surrender to

our bodies like the sounds of this early dawn
the moon & you & I

wild fragrance & our kisses
will overthrow time

PROPHECY CONCERNING OPPOSITES

victory will arrive
no longer caring about defeat

happiness will exist without
being metamorphosized from misery

Consciousness will now invent for the first time
the movement of History

IMAGES

a vision
of world madness
or of flowers
dancing
with my
Eyes

a unicorn
the color of the
Evening Star
sitting on a red blanket

your fingers
slowly
on my head
& your Eyes
being
always the Sky

TO THE WOMEN AT BEDFORD PRISON

you supreme judges
who vomit words of icebergs
you lawyers with mouths

of quicksand sinking deeper
into your fingers gouging coins
you doctors with your psycho fingers

inciting even the stems
of the hibiscus to screech
out to the snow black moon for relief

you critics
who daily declare the
Quarter Moon impotent

you bearded prophets
from jerusalem who pretend to come
on cia roasted nuts

you lonely men & women
who dream of love
of bodies clutching yourselves

you people
with no place to go

who dream so secretly
that you have no knowledge
of your dreams

& you poets who imagine
children in red parks

who write poems in subway
stops while your minds

disintegrate into miles of words
as rats run up & down
shrieking at the train

& you poets who believe in hope
as much as in tomorrow's rising sun

you sentimental political poets
you romantic poets

you poets who stay up
all night eating tv

you poets who listen to music
who eat music
who get up & begin to dance with yourselves

& you body & tongue poets
who dream of licking yourselves

you horsethieves who moan
about sister & brother hoods
but never sing of love

you cynics & skeptics who believe
the world is illusory
but hunger for a friend's face to touch

you eagles who threaten
to sue me because I desire
to fly higher than you in the sky

& you mountains
who complain endlessly against me
because I'm about to climb onto your nipple peaks

Listen to me

       I will take all of you
       into my body

       I will undress you together
       & myself

       I will reveal your secrets to yourselves
       I will teach you to respect your dreams

       my Eyes
       will eat all of your unfinished thoughts

       I will bathe you
       in the Euphrates with my tongue

       I will feed you songs of prophecy
       until you learn to love me
       until you are reborn

FRAGMENTS OF A PLAN TO
MURDER MY MEMORY

love & sentimentality
have nothing in common
except that they are at odds

love strives to be whole
to be reborn each day

sentiment is concerned
only with the past
the future is included only surreptitiously

that what was
& is dead
must be made to exist again

memory – you play me for a fool
I listen to a song
look at an old face

for a moment
you transport me
into a past oozing with senile sunsets

you push me back upon
what was
using the present to indulge

my avid fantasies
you institutionalize
my naked body & strangle my mind

yet in spite of what you try to do
you will lose memory
I will demolish you

the way time crushes carbon
& evaporates the imagination of rock

only I will do it quickly
I will dismantle your atomic structure now

I will tie you to a mountain
with a chain of green fire

vultures from heaven
will eat all of you
gnaw each atom of your past

today the world is new
I am new

to this moment when your touch
expels any residual fear
left inside me

to this instant of the world spinning
when with your hands you take all of me
& time comes to a halt

to this time
when you & I conscious
of our Eyes meet

Intuition & the Moon
becoming
one another

THE POET AT AGE FOUR

young Poet
staring at an old camera
in your sailor suit

even at four
you were losing
your hair

I can see how large your Eyes are
like moon craters
reflecting all the sun

from Eyes
as large as yours
I see a Poet

who will write about
himself as a boy
who will touch & look

at himself at four
whose Eyes are already the
sky's morning stars

TO EVENING

        daughter in my August dreams

your eyes are like the sound
of poplars hugging orchids of rain

or when a glass full of wind
consumes my face

your eyes are when
the Imagination
invents a wild lotus to sing with

TO IISHA

Little Black haired
girl

'IIsha is my name'
        you told me as I walked by & said hello

dreams floated out of your mouth
& touched my eye as you spoke

'IIsha is my name
 I'm giving a concert tonight'

Little Black IIsha
barely five

you were so free
you took my hand

caution was not in your mind
& we would have danced just then

but for a woman   very big
who peered out a door & began to scream

'IIsha – what are you doing
 don't you know yet
 not to be talking to strangers'

you were still smiling at me
as the woman   very big

scooped you up in front of me
& shoved you into a narrow hallway
kicking the door shut

I stood outside the doorway for a while
then walked away

Little Black haired child
I'll remember you
we were about to dance

AMERICA: A VISION

I

in the clouds
a green wind moves over you
sent by the Imagination
to determine what in you is redeemable

listen
this is the wind's warning

        wake up wake up
        wake up from your bad dreams
        taste yourself
        discover your body cut off from its mind
        where is your mind America

II

it is easier to love you here
in the clouds
than in the city streets of New York
        or Philadelphia or Boston

do not think it is only because
you have gotten fatter
that the night air curses you
& the moon waits patiently for her revenge

at birth you had imagined yourself a songwriter
& so you began

        "when in the course of human events. . ."

it was a good beginning
you were aware at least that history is
the history of human intentions
but there your song ended

you promised equality
but only so long as it was man's
& man only as he was white
& white only if wealthy

your song became a lamentation instead
you spit on Imagination
replaced it with black slavery
& woman's subjugation

III

wake up America
wake up from your nightmare
taste yourself
discover your body in a thousand pieces
rolling through city dumps

your mind – where is your mind America

smell the earth that surrounds you
it was good once
see how the fragrance of the red cactus
has become tar

what are you at 200
do you believe you can continue to grow fat

plagues & hydras will devastate you
quagmires & blue lepers will smash your face

Listen to me now America

      you will take Imagination & embrace & kiss it
      lick & heal it

      you will feed all hungry faces & inventors
      of your eyes

you will transform yourself
into a being that thinks

you will gather eucalyptus leaves
& wild herbs

you will purify yourself
you will undress & bathe with earth & sky

the wind Poets fly on will suck you
until you are dry

take the cactus & wild herbs
rub them deeply into yourself

now learn your birth promises
rethink your past
recall the visions you once sang about

reinvent your body
discover your mind

you will do this now America
drink the Poet's milk of vision

disrobe touch yourself
dismantle the tar

discover your mind
reinvent yourself now

THE CORRECT WAY TO THROW ORANGE JUICE

I

you in your pin stripe wide tie
starch can suit
& I have lunch time talk
walking on first avenue

on the balcony across the street
you begin looking
at the way she is sitting

"look at her cunt" you yell
shoving your hands inside your pants
it is your laughter I despise

II

I walk beside you
arguing at sidewalks & walls
wondering how I will be able to work
in the same office we will go back to

I am carrying a container of juice
half–full in my left hand

you feel you must make a point about sex
so you mention Malcolm X
as you begin to move your mouth
a stranger creeps by in a steel hat

"Malcolm X was just another nigger"
the steel head shouts

I am drowned by words refusing to move
until my tongue wound like a spring
explodes in his fat comfortable face

calling him a rude piece of shit
has only limited success
as momentary as a sneeze

it is only when I empty this container of juice
half-full over his bald white steel head
down the hole in his nose on his fat face

that he begins to move away
poking his fingers in the sky
smashing the afternoon air

III

the steel head gone I look at you again
I am holding the container
I look inside   it is empty

you glance at me
but you are a diplomat so you smile
like an insect before clearing its throat

back in the office I watch numbly
as secretaries praise you for your kindness
your good humor as you ask if they
would like some coffee   no bother you say

IV

you are completely unaware of yourself
a dead past a relic like primogeniture
your eyes are a scar on the wind

you are dying but you will be the last to know
you will die believing it is only a bad dream

when you die worms will eat your blue mouth
when you die the wind will laugh

MAXIM FOR POETS MURDERED

I

a revolutionary movement
lacking a
Sense of Humor
will always fail

II

never trust anyone
who is afraid to
Laugh
when others won't

TO A TREE

there you wait tree
enclosed by ten floors of angry steel

shouting hysterically at you
& all you can do

is hope for a cool wind
to lick you as it flies by

better to be hacked to death
than live any longer chained

better to escape   fly away
blow the building down

than squirm for the right
to pay for a scrap of the sun

TO ALL SKEPTICS & MASOCHISTS

I invite you to kiss yourself
to let your dreams become your body

touch her breast
do you still doubt the World

then I invite you to
taste the wind & the color of thighs

to invent your face
& look at my Eyes

they are the history of sound
of all desires that will ever be

I invite you to stay a while
to touch my Eyes

I invite the lakes & seas of your invisible mouth
to rise & discover the sky

to kiss my body
to hold history in your hands

LUST

lust which sweeps
me away
like an Antarctic breeze

carrying the aroma of wild lilacs
lust which my body breathes
in deeply like cold air

in a Vermont sky
& my Eyes shut tight
like a vault preserving titanium

dreams in the night
craving deeper in me
than any bee's search

for crocus blossoms
a lure
which like the early tides

the moon causes
endlessly tugging at the earth
I satisfy as if a physical law

which cannot be negated
without denying sparrows fly

or the January wolf moon
in a red sky

LOVE POEM

if in the mist
        of morning stars
you touch my brows

if when the sun
        is the red
of sky

& your night songs
        purify the air
I breathe

if in quick time
        language is transmuted
& beauty no longer kept from flower

if when our body
        touches at last
our Imagination of knowing

& thought
        gives way
to thighs

if when eyes
          are
no longer false

& Intuition
          no slower
than the speed of light

if then
          in the
midst of morning stars

we touch brows
          & all eyes
finally hear

love will be like
          a song
the wind dreams of

flying to flutes
          undressing
on hillsides

THURSDAY EVENING IN GUATEMALA

breeze on my lips
watching your thighs
in between
Lake Atitlan & volcano

slight rain falls
as I listen to
summer dismantle the sky

I see you there alone
holding your face

I imagine undressing your mouth
dissolving your face
eating your apple face

removing the silence from your hips
of pouring blue songs
through each miraculous nipple

tasting your ears
where purple thunder grows

licking your legs
where the afternoon sleeps

boring through your skin of roses
to the other side of sound
of swimming to your panther eyes

where suns reflect the color
of your morning desire

TO THE WOMAN WHO SMILED

you smile as I walk by
a sun
kissing my every bone

I would give you this
large blue magnolia leaf
I would love your both eyes

one orange
the other fuchsia
I would love you here now

in the Arboretum
above the *tibouchina laxa*

only you are holding his thigh
I imagine kissing
your thin mouth

& dream
a million prehistoric leaves falling

turning white
laughing

you will smile again
& all the trees will bow

PROPHECY: A VISION

there will come a time
when Poetry & History
will embrace

& when at last
this time does arrive
Poets will have made

their last prophecy
there will no longer
be a need

for Intuition
to issue bulletins
concerning fate

history will unbolt its mind
professors will throw
themselves in the sea

Imagination
will restore philosophy

the choice between
eyes & truth will always be a lie

there will come a time
when Poetry & History
will embrace

UNTITLED

the
     flying
         to
             heaven
                  will
                     always
                          be
                             your
                                 eyes

KOSROF CHANTIKIAN, of Armenian descent, was
born in his mother's bed in her home in Cuba at 6am
on 27 January 1943. He moved to New York City
at the age of four where he lived most of his
life. On 4 July 76, he arrived in San Francisco.

He fell from grace at seventeen by studying
electrical engineering, began to climb out of
the abyss through mathematics, found his way
with philosophy & finally at thirty, redeemed
& invented himself as Word–Dreamer & Poet.

His first book of poetry, *Imaginations &
Self-Discoveries*, was published in 1974.
He is editor of *Kosmos*: A Journal of Poetry.